Detector Dog

Written by John Parsons

Rigby

Chapter Snapshots

1. Sniffing for Clues Page 4

Dogs have a better sense of smell than we do. At airports around the world, we use their sense of smell to keep our countries safe.

2. Meet Taffy Page 10

Taffy is an Australian detector dog, and Miriam is her handler. Together they work to prevent unsafe plants, animals, and foods from entering Australia.

"Quarantine detector

3. Taffy is Rewarded Page 20

Taffy finds a prohibited item.
She is rewarded with a special treat!

4. A Lucky Dog Page 28

Taffy has an important
job and is well looked
after — but she hasn't
always been so lucky.

dogs are like detectives."

1. Sniffing For Clues

Dogs have a better sense of smell than we do. But do you know why?

4

Both dogs and people have scent receptors in their noses. Scent receptors let us smell things.

Dogs have *millions* more scent receptors than us!

Scent Receptors

A scent receptor looks like this.

What's in a Nose?

A dog has about 220 million scent receptors in its nose. A human nose only has about 10 million scent receptors in it.

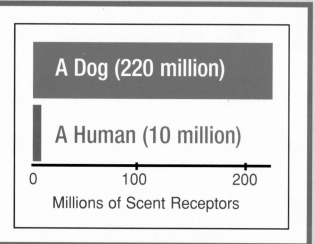

A Dog (220 million)

A Human (10 million)

0   100   200

Millions of Scent Receptors

Dogs use their sense of smell in many ways. They sniff the scents of other dogs and people.

At some airports around the world, we use dogs' amazing sense of smell to keep countries safe from illegal drugs and currency.

In Australia, special "detector dogs" are used at airports to find unsafe plants, animals, and foods.

Australian quarantine detector dogs are like detectives. They look for clues we cannot easily see, hear, taste, smell, or touch. The clues may be hidden in passengers' bags.

In Australia, passengers arriving at the airport must report any food, plant, or animal materials to the customs officers who run the Quarantine and Inspection Service.

Declare it to

You must declare anything made from plants wooden articles, dairy products, meat products, as well as live animals.

Quarantine

Quarantine

or animals, including
fresh fruit, seeds and nuts,

Matters!

2. Meet Taffy

Taffy is a quarantine detector dog at an Australian airport. She has an important job, helping to protect the country against plant and animal diseases.

Miriam is Taffy's handler. Together they check thousands of bags, boxes, and suitcases every week.

Miriam and Taffy work for the Australian Quarantine and Inspection Service.

How Are Detector Dogs Chosen?

Some dogs, such as beagles, have better scent receptors than others. Detector dogs must also be friendly, and show no aggression toward people. They need to feel comfortable in noisy and busy places, such as airports. Like most dogs they want to work hard to get a reward — usually a food treat!

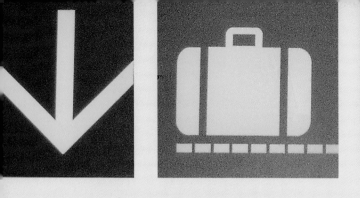
Taffy and Miriam start
work early. The first plane
to arrive in Australia from
overseas lands at about
4:30 a.m.

Within minutes, the
passengers' bags, boxes,
and suitcases from the
plane are brought into
the airport.

12

A Working Team

Ever since Taffy started training as a quarantine detector dog, she has worked with Miriam. Miriam is responsible for Taffy's grooming, exercise, and feeding. They work well as a team and are good friends. It's a great job for both of them, and Miriam says she loves it!

Follow me and my paw prints. I can smell something unsafe.

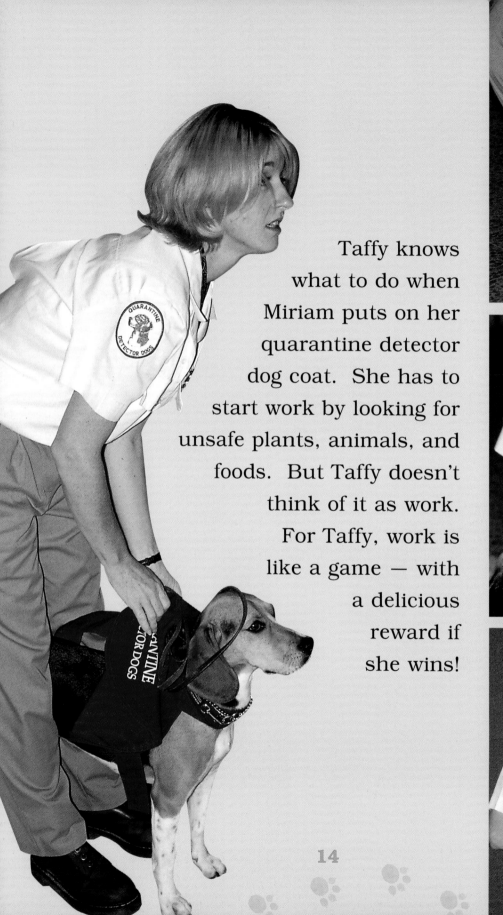

Taffy knows what to do when Miriam puts on her quarantine detector dog coat. She has to start work by looking for unsafe plants, animals, and foods. But Taffy doesn't think of it as work. For Taffy, work is like a game — with a delicious reward if she wins!

14

Why Are Some Plants, Animals, and Foods Unsafe?

Plants, animals, and foods may have diseases or pests in them that are foreign to Australia.

For example, if fruit with a foreign disease is brought into the country, the disease could spread to all fruit trees. Australian fruit growers would have to throw away their fruit and lose millions of dollars.

As passengers and their bags arrive at the airport, Taffy has been trained to sniff out many things.

	Fresh fruit and vegetables
	Meat, even if it is inside a can
	Plants and parts of plants, like flowers
	Other animal and plant material, like eggs and seeds
	Reptiles, like lizards and snakes
	Bees
	Other live animals, like birds

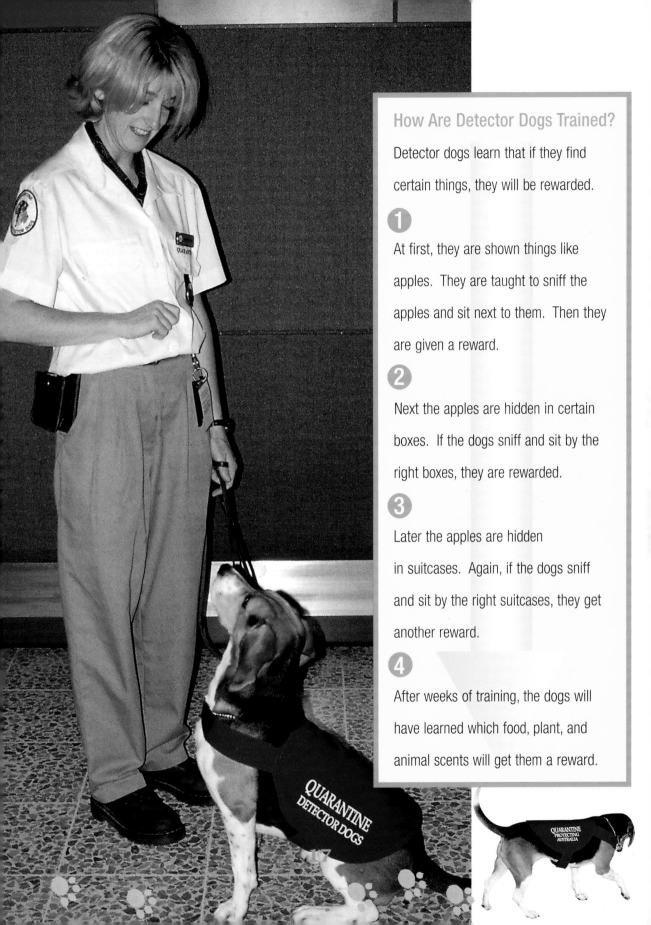

How Are Detector Dogs Trained?

Detector dogs learn that if they find certain things, they will be rewarded.

1

At first, they are shown things like apples. They are taught to sniff the apples and sit next to them. Then they are given a reward.

2

Next the apples are hidden in certain boxes. If the dogs sniff and sit by the right boxes, they are rewarded.

3

Later the apples are hidden in suitcases. Again, if the dogs sniff and sit by the right suitcases, they get another reward.

4

After weeks of training, the dogs will have learned which food, plant, and animal scents will get them a reward.

Miriam waits while Taffy quickly sniffs a passenger's bag.

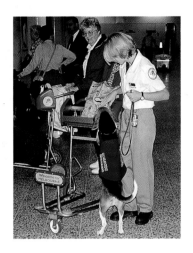  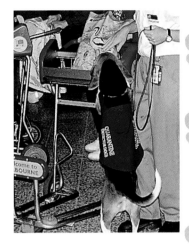

Some passengers want to pat or play with Taffy. But most people leave her alone. They know that she has an important job to do.

Taffy has been trained to ignore the passengers and the noise. All Taffy wants to do is find something that will get her a reward!

19

3. Taffy Is Rewarded

Suddenly, from all the scents that surround her, Taffy smells something! Finally, she may get her reward!

She pushes her nose closer to a passenger's bag. She sniffs deeply. She has smelled some apples!

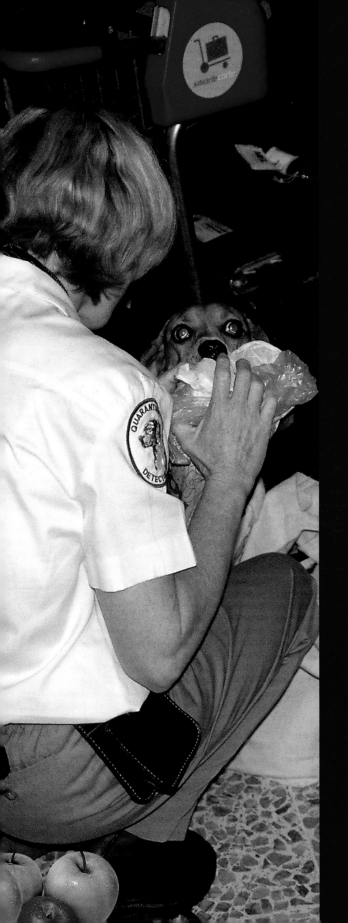

Instantly, Taffy sits down.
This is her sign
to Miriam that she has
found a prohibited item.

Miriam crouches down
behind Taffy. She does
this to protect Taffy's tail
from people stepping on it.

Then Miriam politely asks
the passenger if there are
any plants, animals,
or food in their bag.

Miriam looks inside the bag and finds some apples. They are prohibited items, so Miriam explains to the passenger that the apples must be taken away.

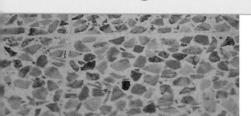

As Taffy has done her job well, she is rewarded with a special food treat. Then Miriam pats and plays with Taffy.

Taffy knows that every time she finds a prohibited item, she will be treated like this — so she always does her best!

What Happens to Prohibited Items?

Prohibited items, such as apples, are put in a special trash container. Later that day, everything in the container will be buried in a deep hole.

By burying the items, no new foreign diseases or pests will escape to destroy Australian fruit trees and other plants.

Declare it to Quarantine

Don't risk a fine over $100 or prosecution

QuarantineMatters!

RED EXIT

Goods to Declare

←

GREEN EXIT

Nothing to Declare

→

Taffy and Miriam have checked all the bags from this flight. Only the apples were found.

Most of the passengers have picked up their bags. Before they leave the airport, they must go through one last check.

If the passengers have items or goods to declare in their bags, they walk through the red exit. A quarantine officer will check that the items are safe.

If the passengers have nothing to declare, they take the green exit.

24

Once all the passengers have left, Miriam takes Taffy's coat off. Taffy knows that her sniffing job is over for a while.

The next plane arrives in ten minutes. Until then, Taffy and Miriam enjoy a little game.

Uniforms

Quarantine detector dogs always wear their coats while working, and their handlers always wear a uniform. Their uniforms clearly show passengers that they work for the Australian Quarantine And Inspection Service. Detector dog handlers also wear a "Quarantine Detector Dogs" badge.

QUARANTINE DETECTOR DOGS

What's Unusual?

Some Unusual Items!

Some passengers from overseas may not know that some of the things they are bringing into Australia are unsafe. The Australian quarantine detector dogs and the Quarantine And Inspection Service staff have found many unusual items.

Just imagine finding …

- musical instruments with thousands of tiny **bugs** in them

- stuffed animals, such as **bats**

- bottles filled with dead animals, such as **squid**

- picture frames filled with **seeds**

- pine cones

Bugs

Bats

Squid

Seeds

Pine Cones

26

What's Allowed?

Some foods, animal items, and plant items may be allowed into Australia if they don't have any pests or diseases. Australian quarantine staff must check everything. Some items may need to be specially treated to kill hidden insects. Some different types of food, animal, and plant items are listed below.

Items to Inspect and Treat

Food
- Cookies and cakes
- Chocolate
- Honey

Animal Items
- Feathers and seashells
- Leather and skins

Plant Items
- Cane baskets
- Straw dolls

KEY

MUST BE INSPECTED

MUST BE TREATED

4. A Lucky Dog

By finding the apples, Taffy may have saved the country's apple trees from a dangerous apple disease.

But the best part of Taffy's story is that she, too, was saved.

Before Taffy became a detector dog, she had been left at a lost dogs' home. No one wanted her.

Taffy was a lonely puppy until she was rescued by the Australian Quarantine And Inspection Service. Luckily, they knew that beagles were clever dogs.

Now Taffy has an important job and she is well taken care of. She is a lucky dog — but thousands of Australian people are lucky, too. They need to grow and sell high-quality fruit, vegetables, meat, plants, and animals to make money.

With dogs like Taffy on the job, their jobs are safe!

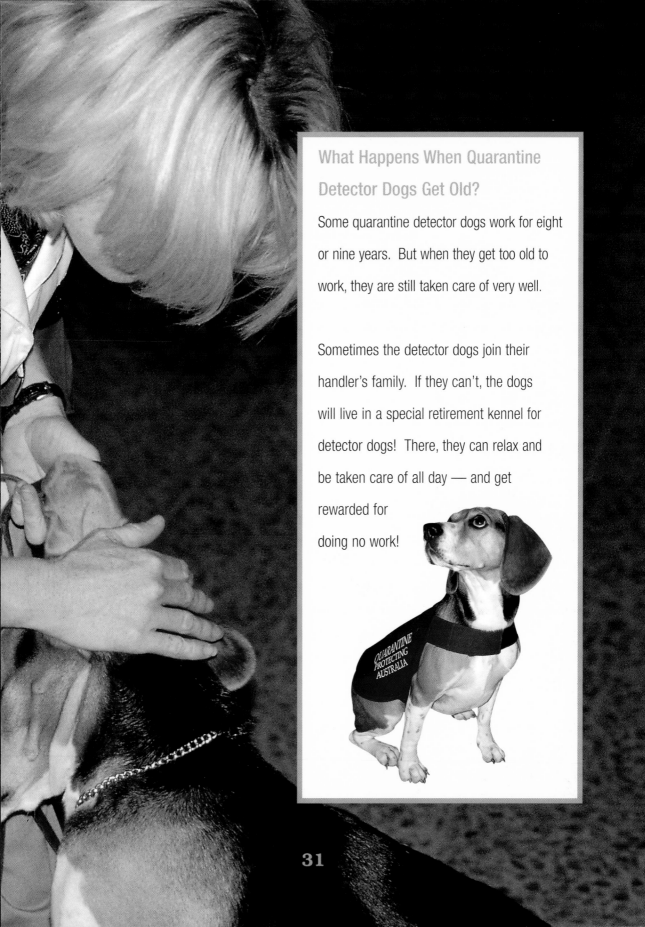

What Happens When Quarantine Detector Dogs Get Old?

Some quarantine detector dogs work for eight or nine years. But when they get too old to work, they are still taken care of very well.

Sometimes the detector dogs join their handler's family. If they can't, the dogs will live in a special retirement kennel for detector dogs! There, they can relax and be taken care of all day — and get rewarded for doing no work!

Index

Bookweb Links

Read more Bookweb 3 books about dogs, senses, and airports!

Ready for Take-Off! — Nonfiction

Sensational! — Nonfiction

I Spy! — Nonfiction

Optometrist — Nonfiction

The Dog's Guide to Humans — Fiction

And here's another Bookweb 3 book about a detective!

Inspector Grub and the Jelly Bean Robber — Fiction

Key To Bookweb Fact Boxes

☐ Arts

☐ Health

☐ Science

☐ Social Studies

☐ Technology